THIS BOOK IS ANTI-RACIST
Journal

Frances Lincoln
Children's Books

Dear Reader,

Thank you for picking up this journal! I am so excited to share this with you and to be part of your journey into becoming anti-racist. Remember, this is lifelong work. Within these pages you will find some familiar information. You will also find many new reflections, activities and prompts. There's space for you to learn and grow. I've been wanting to share a journal with you from the very beginning and I hope you will find yourself inside this book. I hope you will continue to stay awake, start taking action and always lean into the work of disrupting racism.

We have seen since *This Book Is Anti-Racist* was published in January 2020, that our world continues to wake up. I continue to write with a heart filled with grief for Breonna Taylor, George Floyd, Tyree Davis, Kwame Jones, Atatiana Jefferson, Micah Lee, Mubarak Soulemane, Queasha D Hardy, Abdirahman Salad, Elijah McClain, Barry Gedeus, Darrell William Mobley Sr., Daniel Prude, Aerrion Burnett, and Ahmaud Arbery. Too many folx continue to become our ancestors. Families, schools, organizations, and some countries are starting to understand the importance of learning about racism and doing the work to disrupt it.

Racism is not a thing of the past. It is still here and, as long as we have breath in our lungs, we have to fight for justice. Together, we can abolish the system that continues to misuse and abuse power and collectively work for anti-racism.

This journey begins with you and we are in this together.

In solidarity,

Tiffany

(she/her)

"IN A RACIST SOCIETY IT'S NOT ENOUGH TO BE NON RACIST WE MUST BE ANTI-RACIST"

3

THIS IS ME ON THIS DAY!

(Add a photo of you or illustrate yourself.)

Name (as you like to be called) and your pronouns:

_____

Age:

_____

Where you are:

_____

_____

Today's date:

_____

This is the day you are starting on your journey into anti-racism!

Before we begin, let's take a moment to learn about this land you reside on...

Write on!

Where I live is currently called:

_____

_____

The indigenous group(s) who call this land home is/are:

_____

_____

This land was originally called:

_____

_____

Some things I'd like to know more of about the land I live on:

_____

_____

_____

_____

You may use the NativeLand app or start a search online that begins with "Who were the first inhabitants of [name of your city, country here.]" Sometimes it's easy to find this information and sometimes you have to do a little extra digging! You may also reach out to your local historical society and talk to elders in your community. They have a lot of information about the history of where you live!

I currently live on the traditional lands of the Nipmuck and Pocumtuc. If you live in Ontario, Canada, you are on the unceded territory of the Cree, Anishinabek, and the Métis. If you are in Sydney, Australia, you are on Eora land. If you live in Chicago, Illinois in the US you are on the land that the Miami and the Potawatomi folx call home. If you are in Kiruna, Sweden, you are inhabiting Sápmi, home to the Sámi people. If you live in Santo Domingo, Dominican Republic, you are residing on the traditional lands of the Taíno. And, if you live in Asuncíon, Paraguay, you are on the land of the Guaraní people.

Learning about the land we live on will help us to, not only acknowledge the past, but become better stewards (caretakers) so those who come long after us will have this earth. Learning about the original names of my city, and what happened to the indigenous tribes of the Nipmuck and Pocumtuc when English settlers colonized and dominated the land and people, has deepened my understanding of how the work of racism and colonization is not new. It happens everywhere. No place is immune to the effects of racism and colonization.

While the colonizers made an effort to erase the names of people and their land, please know that people indigenous to your home are not people of the past, they are people of today, and of the future, and even seven generations still to come.

> *"THIS LIFE IS A GIFT AND IT IS OUR RESPONSIBILITY TO RESPECT AND PROTECT THAT WHICH GIVES US LIFE."*

Xiuhtezcatl Roske-Martinez shared in his address at the 2015 United Nations general assembly. He is an environmental activist, hip-hop artist, and director of the organization Earth Guardians, who shares his indigenous roots to stand up and speak out about climate change and the human impact on our earth. He has been doing this since he was 6 years old.

Use this space to collect your questions, thoughts, ideas, words, images, anything, and everything.

Get creative!

Let's pause and reflect.

Set some guidelines for yourself.
What do you value? What do you believe?
Make a list!

_____

_____

_____

_____

_____

_____

_____

Values are things that are important to you. They help to guide you in what you do in your life.

How will these values keep you anchored when the work of anti-racism feels overwhelming, enraging, and exciting?

Some of the things I value are: truth, community, and joy. We may have similar things on our list, or they may be completely different.

What do you need in order to learn and grow? Think of what materials and supplies you may want and need.

- Who are the folx that you can trust and rely on?
- Who will help you and encourage you to be brave and become anti-racist?

Your anti-racist vision.

What will it look like, feel like, and be like when we eradicate the structures of racism? (They are cracking and crumbling, can you feel it?) What will our communities look like without racism? How do you envision we will get there? What will your role be? Will it stay the same? How will you grow and change and transform in this vision?

Create a clear vision of what it is you're working towards. This will keep you focused, so you are spending your time and energy with intention.

SET A TIMER FOR FIVE MINUTES AND GO!

I am...

You are not solely defined by your social identities.
They are the parts of you that relate to other people in society.
These categories—and the way you define yourself within
them—are based on creations that have been named, framed,
and defined by society over the course of a long time.

(This list does not include everything and does not
show a complete picture of who you are.)

SOCIAL IDENTITY CATEGORIES

- RACE
- ETHNICITY
- SOCIOECONOMIC CLASS
- GENDER EXPRESSION
- SEXUAL ORIENTATION
- AGE
- NATIONALITY
- LANGUAGE
- RELIGIOUS BELIEFS
- ABILITIES
- EDUCATION
- FAMILY STRUCTURE

Then, there are your personal identities. These are the parts of you that you define, create, name, and frame.

What do you sound like?

Favorite color?

What do you like to do?

How do you feel?

Favorite animal?

When is your birthday?

Favorite shape?

Who are your friends?

What do you like to eat?

Where is your favorite place to be?

Write your own questions here:

_____

_____

Activist and philanthropist, and "future president" [of the United States], **Mari Copeny** (also known as Little Miss Flint) has been advocating for environmental and racial justice since she was 8-years-old and shares this advice:

"IF THEY DON'T WANT TO LISTEN TO YOU AT FIRST, KEEP ON TALKING, THEY WILL EVENTUALLY HAVE TO HEAR YOU OUT. AND ONCE THEY HEAR YOU OUT, THEY WILL SEE THAT YOU HAVE A UNIQUE VIEW OF THE WORLD AND THAT YOUR OPINION MATTERS."

This is a map of you. It shows who you are as a whole person!

Place your name at the center. Then, all around, write, draw, collage, stick, and paint your many and various identities.

Get creative!

Build your map however you would like. You may want to keep coming back to this to add more details of who you are.

How diverse is your universe?

(There's space to add your own categories at the end.)

Write down—if you know—the race and ethnicity of the people in your life (and you can do this with your other social identities, too):

Write on!

I am

_____

My family members are

_____

My closest friends are

_____

The neighbors on our block are

_____

My doctor is

_____

My dentist is

_____

Most of my teachers are
(If you are homeschooled or unschooled, think about the groups you connect with and the folx who lead those groups.)

_____

My favorite teacher is

_____

The principal is

_____

Most of the other people in my class are

_____

The characters in my favorite TV show or movie are

_____

The last author I read is

_____

_____

_____

REFLECT: What do you notice about your "universe"?

Here, you can place the parts of you that you may not be ready to reveal!

Glue an envelope here.

IT'S TIME FOR A CHECK-IN!

Right now, at this very moment, how are you feeling? What do you know right now that you didn't know before you started working in this journal?

IMAGINARY BOX

DOMINANT CULTURE

Let's explore the dominant culture.

The dominant culture has created a "normal" (or status quo) that has shaped how we see ourselves and the world around us; it is the group of people in a country who hold the most power and are often (but not always) in the majority. Check-in on pages 12 and 17 of *This Book Is Anti-Racist*.

1. Which identities are inside the "imaginary box" of the dominant culture? (Place these inside the box.)

2. Which identities are outside the box, and <u>not</u> a part of the dominant culture? (Place these outside and all around the box.)

3. Are there parts of you that are inside the box? Circle/underline/star/highlight them.

4. Are there identities you hold that are outside of the box? Circle/underline/star/highlight them.

5. Notice which parts of you are inside the box and which are outside. You may be completely outside the box or totally inside the box.

Use this space to collect words that inspire, energize, and empower you!

If you could spend time with any anti-racist changemaker (living or no longer with us), who would you spend time with? What would you talk with them about?

_____

_____

_____

_____

_____

_____

_____

_____

RACE

ETHNICITY

Race is a category that was constructed to identify people based on melanin, hair texture, facial features, and cultural heritage. (Melanin is the pigment in our skin that protects us from the UV rays of the sun. Folks with Global Majority ancestry often have darker melanin than those with European ancestry.)

It started as a hierarchy with Caucasian at the top. ("The most beautiful form.") Remember, this is an opinion, it's **not** based in fact.

Race and ethnicity are not the same, but often get lumped together.

Your cultural heritage: Languages, traditions, ancestral history

Examples of ethnicity:
*   Japanese American
*   Zapotec
*   Caribbean British
*   African American
*   Navajo
*   Sudanese Australian

MY RACE:

MY ETHNICITY:

Take a deep breath... pause... and reflect...

What do you know about your ethnic identity?

_____

_____

Is this something you think and talk about often?

_____

_____

What do you know about your racial identity?

_____

_____

Is this something you think and talk about often?

_____

_____

_____

_____

It's time to create some affirmations for yourself because **YOU ARE AMAZING!**

An affirmation is a positive statement that will remind you that you are strong, brave, smart, fun, and powerful (among many, many other things.)

You may also want to tear them out of this journal and carry them around with you, tape them up so you can see them every day, or share them with others.

WRITE YOUR AFFIRMATIONS DOWN HERE.

RACISM IS PERSONAL PREJUDICE AND BIAS AND THE SYSTEMIC MISUSE AND ABUSE OF POWER BY INSTITUTIONS

Color in!

Here, reflect on and finish the statement:

"WHAT I KNOW ABOUT RACISM..."

What do you want to know more about?

What are you learning?

_____

_____

_____

_____

_____

_____

_____

_____

_____

"RACE AND RACISM IS A REALITY THAT SO MANY OF US GROW UP LEARNING TO JUST DEAL WITH. BUT IF WE EVER HOPE TO MOVE PAST IT, IT CAN'T JUST BE ON PEOPLE OF COLOR TO DEAL WITH IT. IT'S UP TO ALL OF US — BLACK, WHITE, EVERYONE — NO MATTER HOW WELL-MEANING WE THINK WE MIGHT BE, TO DO THE HONEST, UNCOMFORTABLE WORK OF ROOTING IT OUT."

- MICHELLE OBAMA

REFLECTING ON POWER.

Explore power.

What is power? What does it look like, smell like, feel like, sound like, and taste like?

You might want to draw, write, dance, sing, cook, move, meditate, and so on, to do this exploration.

Who holds power?

Notice who has power. Notice their race and whether they are a part of the dominant culture.

Who is the head of your school?

_____

Who runs the biggest corporations?

_____

Who are your teachers?

_____

Who runs the country? The state?

_____

Who are the celebrities you see often? Who is in the shows and movies you watch?

_____

Who are the authors you read at school? Who are the authors you choose to read?

_____

What other questions can you ask?

What power do these institutions hold?

- Government
- Media and entertainment
- Business
- Housing
- Banks
- Criminal justice system
- Education
- Health care

Specifically, what power regarding race and racism do these institutions hold?

For example: Banks give loans to people so they can buy homes.

What power does each institution hold?

Who runs these institutions?

How do they/could they misuse and abuse power?

How could they use their power for racial justice?

Which institutions have a direct impact on you?

_____

_____

_____

_____

How can institutions misuse and abuse their power?

_____

_____

_____

_____

_____

For example: In media and entertainment, adhering to European beauty standards, we typically see people who are white, tall, cisgender, fit/thin, well groomed, etc. as being the normal everyday person.

I love to collect buttons and wear them when I want to share my beliefs, values, and what I stand for.

Use this space to create your own buttons!

BLACK LIVES MATTER

"WHITE PRIVILEGE IS YOUR HISTORY BEING PART OF THE CORE CURRICULUM AND MINE BEING TAUGHT AS AN ELECTIVE."

- Ozy Aloziem

Rewrite the history books!

What would you rather leave out?
What would you like to add in?

LEAVE OUT	ADD IN

Create your timeline of anti-racism and resistance.

The people who write the history books often leave out stories of resistance and those who actively work towards an anti-racist society. Which stories, people, and movements of resistance would you place on a timeline for all to see and know? Where will you start? Are you on this timeline?

Write a letter to your future self.

Share who you are, what your dreams are, what you're learning, and reflect on how you are growing into your anti-racism.

PAUSE FOR A MOMENT AND GET CREATIVE!

Throughout history, movements and organizations for BIPoC folx and those working toward an anti-racist society have used art to share their messages with others.

WE SHALL SURVIVE. WITHOUT A DOUBT

American artist Emory Douglas was the Minister of Culture for the Black Panther Party for over a decade and a prominent graphic artist in the Black empowerment movement.

Use this page
to create
a collage,
illustration,
comic,
watercolor,
etc. What
is your
message?

Keep track of the books you'd like to read, have read, and want to share!

Read
                                                             Shared

☑ *This Book is Anti-Racist*

Use this space as a place to keep track of the resources you're using for your research. You may want to go back to them another day or share them with your friends, the adults in your life, or everyone!

When you are looking at resources, especially ones you found online, ask yourself a few questions to determine whether this is a true and honest resource or whether it's fake information that is put into the world to create quick emotions and growing distrust within you. Just a few (of many) questions you may want to ask:

- Who created this? (Is this a trusted website? Has the author/reporter written articles before? Is it difficult to figure out who created this?)

- Is this on a site that is credible (one that is well-known) or is it from an unsecure website you've never heard of before? (Double check the source if you are unsure.)
- Who is this for? (Who is the intended audience?)
- Is anyone else reporting on this? (If not, why not?)
- How do you feel when reading this? (Do you feel like the writer is trying to present facts? Or, are they trying to create an emotional reaction in you?)

WRITE YOUR OWN HISTORY!

Where does it begin?

(Do you want to begin today? On the day you arrived on this earth? Before you? Does your story begin with your name? Or, the place where you took your first breath?)

What stories from your life have shaped
you into who you are at this moment?

Use this space to collect those stories!

Who are your ancestors?

(An ancestor is someone who came before you. They can be a family member, like your great-great-grandmother or, they can be someone who is not related to you at all.)

Who are your familial ancestors?

_____

_____

_____

_____

Who are the ancestors of anti-racism (who have resisted and fought for justice) who inspire you and that you'd like to know more about?

_____

_____

_____

_____

What is the history of your family?
(How do you define family?)

_____

_____

_____

_____

What are the stories you've always been told
and the ones you want to know more about?

_____

_____

_____

_____

_____

And, what is your history beyond your family?

- Is it related to the land around you?
- What moments in our collective history have had a large impact on you and your family?
- How did those moments contribute to who you are now?

_____

_____

_____

_____

_____

_____

_____

_____

Create your personal timeline of history.

Your history is important. Use some of the prompts on the previous pages to help you reflect on and create a timeline of your own history. Will you add stories from your community and beyond? Will you keep it just for you? Who will join you on this timeline? What will you want to mark from your history to now?

Pause for a moment and reconnect with nature.

- Dig your feet into the grass.
- Pick up a handful of snow.
- Close your eyes and listen to the wind.
- Feel the sun shining on your cheeks.
- Listen for the chirp of a bird, the buzz of an insect, the mew of a kitten.

YOUR SUPER AMAZING SUPERPOWER!

Illustrate a short comic of you using your superpowers to stand up and speak out for anti-racism!

Call in? Call out?

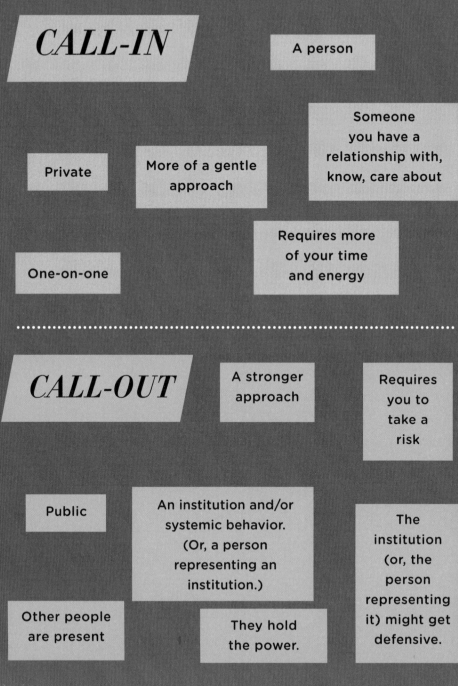

CALL-IN

A person

Someone you have a relationship with, know, care about

Private

More of a gentle approach

Requires more of your time and energy

One-on-one

CALL-OUT

A stronger approach

Requires you to take a risk

Public

An institution and/or systemic behavior. (Or, a person representing an institution.)

The institution (or, the person representing it) might get defensive.

Other people are present

They hold the power.

Before you call in or call out, ask yourself the following questions...they might help you decide how you'll go forth.

- **Who has the power in this situation? The person I'm calling in/out? Or, me?**

  If I have the power - call in.
  If it's not me - call out.

- **Am I calling out a person or systemic behavior?**

  Person - call in.
  Systemic behavior - call out.

- **How much energy and emotional labor am I able to share right now?**

  I can share a lot - call in.
  I'm exhausted - call out.

- **Is this person likely to change their problematic behavior?**

  Yes - call in.
  No - call out.

- **Do I have a relationship with the person or institution?**

  Yes - call in.
  No - call out.

- **Am I centering the needs of myself or of the group?**

  Myself - call in.
  Needs of the group - call out.

- **Am I able and willing to take a risk?**

  Yes - call in.
  No - call out.

Some other questions to consider:

What will happen if I call this behavior out?
What will happen if I call this person in?
What am I hoping to accomplish with this call-in or call-out?

JOY IS HOW WE RESIST!

What is bringing you joy right now?

Make a plan and be ready!

What could you say?

What if...
Your teacher makes a racist comment to another classmate in front of the whole class.

What if...
Your school created a new policy that English must be spoken everywhere other than a language class. You'll get detention if you are not speaking English.

What if...
Your history class uses a textbook that has one paragraph about enslavement in it and labels the enslaved as happy.

What if...
Your friend makes a racist comment at the lunch table and then says "It's just a joke."

What if...
Your teacher continues to mispronounce your friend's name and even once made the comment, "It's just so unusual and ethnic."

What if...
Your teacher keeps assigning books they label as the "classics," which is another way to say— books by old, dead, white British and American guys.

Make a plan.

What could you say?

What if...
A neighbor tells you they believe the country should be closed to "illegals" and immigrants.

What if...
You are at the store and you notice the sales clerk won't help the PoC who is waiting in line and skips over them to attend a white customer.

What if...
Your cousin says "I'm so tired of hearing you say Black Lives Matter. All lives matter."

What if...
You hear someone say "I'm not racist... but..."

What if...
You're talking to a family member and they say, about one of your friends, "She's pretty for a Black girl."

What if...
Someone you don't know asks you, "What are you?" Or, you overhear someone ask another person, "What are you?"

Can you think of other scenarios that might occur in your daily life that you can be ready for?

Will you call in? Or, call out?

If you could go back in time to disrupt a specific historical event, moment or time, what would you choose? What would you do?

Who inspires you to take action?

Winona Guo and **Priya Vulchi,** student activists and founders of CHOOSE, wrote the textbook *Tell Me Who You Are: Sharing Our Stories of Race, Culture, and Identity* because they felt and saw a huge gap in the curriculum they were being taught in school and wanted to address race, justice, intersectionality, and have brave conversations in and out of school.

WINONA GUO & PRIYA VULCHI

TELL ME WHO YOU ARE

SHARING OUR STORIES RACE, CULTURE & TO...

Student activist and community organizer **Zyahna Bryant** organized her first rally when she was 12 years old, for Trayvon Martin. She sparked a national debate in the US calling on the removal of monuments dedicated to Confederate "heroes" (who fought to maintain enslavement in the US during the Civil War.)

ZYAHNA BRYANT

What is in your anti-racist toolbox?

Imagine you are able to have all the things you need to disrupt racism... What are they? Why did you choose these?

Will you share these with others? Will you keep your toolkit to yourself?

Here's what's in mine!

- A notebook and pen so I can write down my observations, thoughts, and more.
- Chocolate and almonds for quick energy.
- Reusable water bottle because I need to stay hydrated.
- Tiger balm because when I'm stressed the tension builds in my shoulders and neck. It hurts and Tiger Balm helps to ease the pain.
- A book to read. (By BIPoC authors and those living outside the imaginary box.)
- My phone (charged!) so I can easily connect, take photos, video, and more.

What will you keep in yours?

YOUR ANTI-RACIST ROUTINE

1. **Wake Up**
   a.   Observe
   b.   Understand who you are
          and who you are growing into

2. **Open the Window**
   a.   Make sense of the world around you
   b.   Know your history

3. **Choose Your Path**
   a.   Take action
   b.   Respond to racism

4. **Hold the Door Open**
   a.   Work in solidarity for anti-racism
   b.   Build relationships
   c.   Take care of yourself

5. *START ALL OVER AGAIN!*

Have you taken action before?

What action did you take? How did you feel?
Were there others with you? What was your role in this?
Would you do this again? Would you do it differently?

Reflecting on taking action:

Was there a time when you wish you had taken action, but did not? Why didn't you? How did this moment contribute to your growth and who you are now?

- What action(s) are you comfortable with?
- What action excites you?
- What action makes you hesitate and pause?

Reflecting on taking action:

- Are you willing and able to go beyond your comfort zone?
- What kind of support do you want/need in order to take action? Who will you do this with?

"I BELIEVE ACTIVISM IS THE TRUE SOURCE OF CHANGE IN THE WORLD. PUSHING TO CHANGE SOCIAL STRUCTURES IN COMMUNITIES THAT YOU ARE A PART OF IS CRITICAL FOR MAKING REAL LASTING CHANGE."

- MARLEY DIAS

Your privilege...

Go back to the imaginary box. Do you have more parts of your whole self to add?

Look at the identities you hold that are a part of the dominant culture. This is where you hold not only privilege, but also power.

Here is where you have agency to work in solidarity with people who do not hold the same privilege and power.

Who do you know (and know of) that fought for and/or is fighting for the abolition of racism and fighting for liberation?

Keep their names here.
Hold their vision for this work in your heart.
Know their work and how they fought in your brain.

You are an ally, an accomplice, and a co-conspirator.

- Get angry. Be upset and outraged. Racism is not okay!
- Keep learning. (How will you continue to do this?)
- Recognize where you hold power and influence, the same with your family. (How can you use this to disrupt racism?)
- What else can you add to this list?

Grow from your discomfort.

Acknowledge your mistakes and grow...
What is a mistake you made when you chose to
stand up and speak out? Or, maybe, you didn't
stand up and speak out...

What will you do differently next time?

_____

_____

_____

_____

_____

_____

_____

_____

TAKE CARE OF YOU...

Who are you?

Who is the you that you will celebrate?

How will you celebrate
you and honor yourself?

Who else will you celebrate?

How will you celebrate and honor others?

What boundaries can and will you set for yourself?

(Because you will get tired and "burn
out" if you try to do everything!)

_____

_____

_____

_____

_____

_____

_____

_____

WHO ARE YOUR PEOPLE?

Let other people hear your voice, know about your journey, and become anti-racist alongside you!

Write a poem, a song, a speech, a letter... write to share with others, just like Amelia Allen Sherwood wrote "Anti-Racist Youth" for you!

Opal Tometi, community organizer, human rights activist, and co-founder of #BlackLivesMatter shared,

"WHAT WE NEED NOW MORE THAN EVER IS A HUMAN RIGHTS MOVEMENT THAT CHALLENGES SYSTEMIC RACISM IN EVERY SINGLE CONTEXT."

We can do this.

KINDNESS WON'T END RACISM.

Stay focused on what you're fighting for. Anti-racism is lifelong work, it doesn't end with this journal.

RESOURCES

Websites to go to for support, information, to learn, and grow:

Black Lives Matter:
https://blacklivesmatter.com/

The Black Curriculum:
https://www.theblackcurriculum.com/

Malala Fund:
https://malala.org/

American Indian College Fund:
https://collegefund.org/

National Indigenous Women's Resource Center:
https://www.niwrc.org/

IllumiNative:
https://illuminatives.org/

National Black Student Alliance:
https://www.nationalbsa.org/

Black Lives Matter at School:
https://www.blacklivesmatteratschool.com/

Coalition for Racial Equality and Rights:
https://www.crer.scot/

Black Visions Collective: https://www.blackvisionsmn.org/

Color of Change:
https://colorofchange.org/

Chicanos por la Causa: https://www.cplc.org/

United We Dream:
https://unitedwedream.org/

NAACP (National Association for the Advancement of Colored People):
https://www.naacp.org/

Race Forward:
https://www.raceforward.org/

Dream Defenders:
https://dreamdefenders.org/

Know Your Rights Camp:
https://www.knowyourrightscamp.com/

Black Youth Project:
https://www.byp100.org/

Fight For Breonna:
https://justiceforbreonna.org/

Trayvon Martin Foundation:
https://www.trayvonmartinfoundation.org/

#SayHerNameCampaign:
https://aapf.org/sayhername

Runnymede:
https://www.runnymedetrust.org/

Black Cultural Archives: https://blackculturalarchives.org/

Stop Hate UK:
https://www.stophateuk.org/

Stephen Lawrence Charitable Trust:
https://www.stephenlawrencetrust.org/

National Council of Asian Pacific Americans:
https://www.ncapaonline.org/

Center for Native American Youth:
https://www.cnay.org/

We R Native:
https://www.wernative.org/

Association on American Indian Affairs:
https://www.indian-affairs.org/

Boat People SOS:
https://www.bpsos.org/

Asian Americans Advancing Justice: https://www.advancingjustice-aajc.org/

Amplifier Art: https://amplifier.org/

Books to read and share:

Nonfiction

Stamped: Racism, Antiracism, and You: A Remix - Jason Reynolds and Ibram X. Kendi

Lifting As We Climb: Black Women's Battle for the Ballot - Evette Dionne

Resist: 35 Profiles of Ordinary People Who Rose Up Against Tyranny and Injustice - Veronica Chambers and Paul Ryding

When They Call You A Terrorist (Young Adult Edition): A Story of Black Lives Matter in the Power to Change the World- Patrisse Khan-Cullors and Asha Bandele, Benee Knauer

We Are Not Yet Equal - Carol Anderson and Tonya Bolden

Black and British: A short essential history - David Olusoga

Making Our Way Home - Blair Imani

Speak Up!: Speeches By Young People to Empower and Inspire - Adora Svitak and Camila Pinheiro

Big Ideas for Young Thinkers - Jamia Wilson and Andrea Pippins

Fiction

Punching the Air - Ibi Zoboi and Yusef Salaam

We Are Not From Here - Jenny Torres Sanchez

Black Brother, Black Brother - Jewell Parker Rhodes

Patron Saints of Nothing - Randy Ribay

Indian No More - Charlene Willing McManis and Traci Sorell

Prairie Lotus - Linda Sue Park

They Called Us Enemy - George Takei

Documentaries and films to watch

When They See Us - Ava DuVernay

Whose Streets? - Sabaah Folayan

"We Are Still Here": A Documentary on Today's Young Native Americans - Emma Li (Imaginesville)

Blacks Britannica - David Koff

NOTES

TIFFANY JEWELL

Tiffany Jewell is a Black biracial writer and AntiRacist Montessori educator and consultant. She spends her time baking bread and macarons, building LEGOS, watching British detective shows, and dreaming up how she can dismantle white supremacy. Tiffany currently

Photo by James Azar Salem

lives in Western Massachusetts with her young activists, her partner, and a turtle she's had since she was nine. This Book Is Anti-Racist was her first book for children and young adults. Find her on instagram: @tiffanymjewell.

AURÉLIA DURAND

Aurélia Durand is a French illustrator based in Paris. Her work is dedicated to representing people of color in society, and she uses bold art as a vivid demonstration. "I use vibrant colors and joyful music to spread good vibes to talk about diversity and open a conversation about why it matters to include more color in

Photo by Aurélia Durand

our society." She wants to create more nuanced illustrative stories by portraying women of color standing proudly and fiercely. Her work has been featured in advertising campaigns, galleries, and editorial magazines. Her clients include Apple, Malala Fund, Urban Decay, Evian, and the New Yorker. She shares her work online on different platforms, mainly Instagram, where she posts daily illustrations, live paintings, and animations. Find her on Instagram: @4ur3lia.

THIS BOOK IS ANTI-RACIST

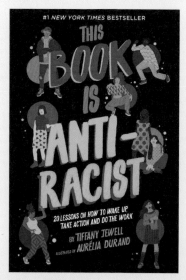

This journal works best when you complete it alongside the original book.

In *This Book Is Anti-Racist*, Tiffany Jewell and Aurélia Durand gave us an essential volume to understand anti-racism.

978-0-7112-4521-1

#1 NEW YORK TIMES BESTSELLER

Featured by Oprah's Book Club on the Anti-Racist Books for Young Adults list curated by bestselling author Jacqueline Woodson

Recommended by *We Need Diverse Books*, *TIME*, *Essence*, *Today*, *Brit + Co*, and *PureWow*.

"A guide to the history of racism and a blueprint for change"
—The Guardian

What is racism? Where does it come from? Why does it exist? What can you do to disrupt it? Learn about social identities, the history of racism and resistance against it, and how you can use your anti-racist lens and voice to move the world toward equity and liberation.

Inspiring | Educating | Creating | Entertaining

Brimming with creative inspiration, how-to projects, and useful information to enrich your everyday life, Quarto Knows is a favorite destination for those pursuing their interests and passions. Visit our site and dig deeper with our books into your area of interest: Quarto Creates, Quarto Cooks, Quarto Homes, Quarto Lives, Quarto Drives, Quarto Explores, Quarto Gifts, or Quarto Kids.

First Published in 2021 by Frances Lincoln Children's Books an imprint of The Quarto Group. Quarto Boston North Shore, 100 Cummings Center, Suite 265D, Beverly, MA 01915, USA, Tel: +1 978-282-9590, Fax: +1 978-283-2742 www.QuartoKnows.com

ISBN 978-0-7112-6303-1

Published by Katie Cotton
Designed by Vanessa Lovegrove and Karissa Santos
Edited by Katy Flint
Production by Dawn Cameron

Manufactured in China

9 8 7 6 5 4 3

MIX
Paper from responsible sources
FSC
www.fsc.org   FSC® C016973

Photo credits: P8: Xiuhtezcatl Martinez, 2016 (Photo by Moses Robinson/Getty Images) P17: Mari Copeny, 2019 (Photo by Noam Galai/Getty Images for Shorty Awards); P34: Michelle Obama, 2019 (Photo by Paras Griffin/Getty Images); P44: © Emory Douglas / DACS 2020; P65: Priya Vulchi and Winona Guo pose with their book, Tell me Who You Are, 2019 in New York City. (Photo by Cindy Ord/Getty Images for Gucci); Zyahna Bryant, 2020 (Photo by Eze Amos/Getty Images); P77: Marley Dias, 2020 (Photo by Elsa/Getty Images).